ABBA FATHER WHY?

WHY HAVE YOU FORSAKEN ME?

By Denise Justice-France

ISBN-13: 978-1503154544

ISBN-10: 1503154548

Abba Father Why?

Why have you forsaken me?

Depression, sickness, when you have feeling of depression, of sickness.
When you feel so alone, when you feel so low, when you feel so
unworthy, when you feel like giving up.

Cry Out!   To the Lord

Cry out Abba Father Why?

Why have you forsaken me?

Pour out your soul to the 'Father"

Tell him it all.
Everything
All your pains, all your hurts.
All your affliciation, all your sorrows,
All your doubts, all your emotions.

Pour out your Soul

Cry Out?   To the Lord

Abba Father Why?
Why have you forsaken me?

Tell him what you are feeling inside,
Tell him what you feel like?

Whether it is good or bad.
Whether it is joy or pain.
Whether it is grief or sorrow.
Whether it is doubt or fear.

Cry Out to the Lord?
Abba Father
Why have you forsaken Me?

Trust the Lord

He is in control, He is in charge

We may not understand Why?

But he does   and he wants to hear if from you.

The Lord was pleased that Solomon had asked for this. So God
said to him "Since you have asked for this and not for long life
or wealth for Yourself.   1 Kings 3:10-11

For Yourself-----   See God said you Ask for Yourself

                              Yes for yourself

We must ask for Yourself-   We must come to the Lord for ourself.

We have a relationship with him.

He is there as our counselor
He is there as our provider.
He is there as our redeemer.
He is our Father. We are His Children.

To cry out to him.   Abba Father,   Why?

As soon as he hears our voice.

His ears Ring, His Face lights up His Glory

Say "Ah Ah" my child calls for me.

He say "Ah Ah" I am here.   "Ah Ah" I hear you.

"AH"   I know all your pain, all your affliction

All your transgression.
"Ah" I know all your Joy.   See we sing when we are happy,

So why not when we are sad.   Tell him

"Abba Father Why?

So God said to him "Since you have asked for this and not for long
    life or wealth for yourself,   1 Kings 3:10-11
      (you can not take nothing with you at death)

nor have asked for the death of your enemies   1 Kings 3:10-11

(prayed for your enemies)

But for discernment in administing justice.   1 Kings 3:10-11

(God will do the justice for us.)

I will do what you have asked.

(What I asked. What I cry out Abba Father Why?)
I cry out to his self, he cry out to the Father in heaven. He became man
for us, to take away all sins. He became us, He became our pain,
our sorrows our affliction, our transgression.   He went to hell for us. He
cry out for us.

He said Abba Father Why have you forsaken me?

I will give you a wise and discerning heart, so that there will never have
been anyone like you, nor will there ever be.   God make us each
different ever one of us, not the same there will never be anyone like you
before never.

Moreover, I will give you what you have not asked,   1 Kings 3:13

(you did not asked to be born) (but I gave you life anyway)

------------------Both riches and honor--------------------- 1 Kings 3:13

(I give you my son)

This is what the Lord says,   He who appoints the sun to shine by day,
who decrees the moon and stars to shine by night, who stirs up the
sea so that its waves roar-------- Jeremiah 31:35
The Lord Almighty is his name.   This what the Lord says:

"Only if the heavens above can be measured and the foundations of the
earth below be searched out will I reject all the descendants of Israel
because of all they have done." declares the Lord.   Jeremiah 31:37

This is the covenant I will make with the house of Israel after   that
times declares the Lord,   "I will put my law in their minds and write it
on their hearts.   I will be their God, and they will be my people,
no longer will a man teach his neighbor or a man his brother, saying
know the Lord, because they will all know me, from the least of
them to the greatest," declares the Lord.

for I will forgive their wickedness and will remember their sins no
more."   Jeremiah 31:33-34

So that in your lifetime you will have no equal among kings. And if you
walk in my ways and obey my statutes and commands as David your
Father did, I will give you a Long Life."   1 Kings 3:13

"Ah, sovereign Lord, you have made heavens and the earth by your
Great Power and out stretched arm, nothing is too hard for you.
You show love to thousands but bring the punishment for the Father'
sins into the laps of their children after them.   (we were born in sin)

O great and powerful God, whose names is the Lord Almighty, great are
your purposes and mighty are your deeds.   Your eyes are open to all the
ways of men you reward everyone according to his conduct and as his
deeds deserve. You performed miraculous signs and wonders in Egypt
and have continued them to this day.   Jeremiah 32

Fall to your knees and Cry out
Abba Father Why? Why have you forsaken me?

Every knee will bow and call on him.

When he saw Jesus, he cried out, and fell down before him, and with a
Loud voice said, "What have I to do with thee, Jesus, thou Son of God
most high? I beseech thee, Torment me not.   Luke 8:28

   (this was a evil spirit talking to Jesus)
   (depression, sickness, lack, doubt, unbelief, fear)

And when he heard that is was Jesus of Nazareth, he began to cry out,
and say, Jesus, thou Son of David, have mercy on me.   Mark 10:47

   (he continued to cry out more)

and many charged him that he should hold his peace, but he cried the
more a great deal, Thou Son of David have mercy on me.   Mark 10:48

and Jesus stood still, and commanded him to be called, and they call the blind man, saying unto him, Be of Good comfort, Rise; he called thee. Mark 10:49

This is what the Lord says, he who made the earth, The Lord who formed it and establish it---- the Lord is his name.
Call to me and I will answer you and tell you great and unsearchable things you do not know.   Jeremiah 33:2

"Here is your king, "Pilate said to the Jews. But they shouted
   "take him away! Take him away! Crucify him!"   John 19:14-15

I am the Good shepherd and I know my own Sheep and they know me, just as my Father knows me and I know the Father; and I lay down my life for the sheep. I have other sheep, too, in another fold. I must bring them also, and they will heed my voice; and there will be one flock with one shepherd.   John 10:14-16

"The Father loves me because I lay down my life that I may have it back again. No one can kill me without my consent--- I lay down my life voluntarily. For I have the right and power to take it again. For the Father has given me this right."   John 10:17-18

(see that's why the said Crucify him?)

Then again the Jewish leaders picked up stones to kill him.
Jesus said " At God's direction I have done many a miracle to help the people. For which one are you killing me?" They replied "Not
for any good work, but for blasphemy, you a mere man, have declared yourself to be God."   John 10.31-33

Jesus replied "the hour has come for the Son of man to be Glorified. I tell you the truth, unless a kernel of wheat falls to the ground and dies, it it remains only a single seed. But if it dies, it produces many seeds. The man who loves his life in this world will lose it, while the man who hates his life in this world will keep it, for eternal life. Whoever serves me must follow me, and where I am, my servant also will be. My Father will honor the one who serves me. "Now my heart is troubled, and what shall I say?

"Father, save from this Hour? No, it was for this very reason I came to this Hour." John 12:23-27

Abba Father? Cry Out Abba Father Why" have you forsaken me?

Father, glorify your Name!" John 12:28

Then a voice from heaven 'I have glorified it, and will glorify it again." John 12:28

And Jesus answered and said unto him, What wilt thou that I should do unto thee? Mark 10:51

The blind man said unto him Lord, that I might received my sight. And Jesus said unto him. "Go they way; thy Faith made thee whole." and Immediately Mark 10:52

He received his sight and followed Jesus in the way.   Mark 10:52

And a lo a voice from Heaven saying
   "this is my beloved Son, in who I am well pleased."   Matthew 3:17

See God will say I am well pleased with you,
   you just cry out to me.

and he said, "Abba Father, all things are possible unto thee; take away
this cup from me; nevertheless not what I will, But what thou wilth.
and said unto them "My soul is exceeding sorrowful unto death; tarry ye
here,a nd watch.   Mark 14:34

Cry Out   "Abba Father   your soul to God the Father.

  he hears, he listens

His son came in our place.

But the scriptures must be fulfilled.   Mark 14:49

And Jesus said I am; and ye shall see the Son of Man sitting on the right
hand of power and coming in the clouds of Heaven.   Mark 14:62

    Abba Father   Abba Father   Abba Father

And that every tongue should confess that Jesus   Lord, to the glory of
God the Father.   Phillipians 2:9

confess Jesus Christ come in flesh in he word son of God.   1 John 4:15

Acknowledgment:

Thank you Lord for this understanding about crying out to you for
Everything, and for not being ashamed to do ask you anything.

You have the ability to express all types of sorrow, pain, suffering,
feeling of doubt, all types of joys to express to you in song, in words of
praise.

Just to come to you as I am and you accept me just as I am. With no
question ASK>

You said Come all you are heavy and burden. Exodus 23:5
You said Come and sing Praises Psalm 150:2

Psalm 150:2English Standard Version (ESV)

2 Praise him for his mighty deeds;
praise him according to his excellent greatness

Thank you Lord for letting me write this.   Thank you.!

Abba Father

Abba Father

Abba Father

Abba Father

Abba Father

Abba Father

Abba Father

Abba Father

www.ingramcontent.com/pod-product-compliance
Lightning Source LLC
Chambersburg PA
CBHW071347310526
45790CB00018B/1381